In Praise of
Letters from Conflict: Poems

"Lisa Stice invokes and addresses war poets past and present in *Letters From Conflict [...]* She evokes the feeling of endless waiting, the visceral absence of a loved one, the worrying, the moving on with life, the elation and disconnect of return, and the joy of small moments during deployment in the poems between the letters. The letters themselves serve as an archive of marginalized voices from wars and historical violence, an archive featuring the voices of predominantly women. Together they make the collection feel like a letter from mother to daughter, one passing on knowledge through storytelling, illumination, and revelation."

—Aly Allen, author of *Paying for Gas with Quarters: A Parent's Odyssey in Poems*

❖ ❖ ❖

"*Letters from Conflict* is one of those wish-I'd-thought-of-that poetry collections, appearing just when we, as readers, have accumulated too many reasons to doubt the ties we have to one another as a community impacted by war. Lisa Stice's poems welcome us all in but offer us some grounded literary history while we're near; we travel from Sun Tzu and Virgil to Lorca and Akhmatova to the poets of today, still holding our mirrors up to war's devastation and to each other. [...]"

—Abby E. Murray, author of *Hail and Farewell: Poems*

❖ ❖ ❖

"In her new book, Lisa Stice writes letters as poems and poems as letters, as a way of connecting with poets from the past. Interspersed among these are poems as journal entries from her own life. Her efforts to bring comfort to these poets of the past serves to simultaneously do the same for us. It's a brave attempt to try to control time in order to give us a little better chance at understanding our own lives. [...]"

—Bill McCloud, author of
The Smell of the Light: Vietnam, 1968-1969

❖   ❖   ❖

Dear Lisa Stice:

A poem is just the right-shaped vial to contain a distilled measure
        of the military,
not too sweet and not too poisonous
but potent and powerful.

These poems are a warning
To my brothers and sisters in arms,
to keep our enemies close but our loved ones closer still;
we may be entertaining poets unawares
and they see everything.

—Nancy Stroer, author of *Playing Army: A Novel*

❖   ❖   ❖

"*Letters from Conflict* knits insistent connections between tender scenes of domestic American life and a kaleidoscope of war survivors and commentators. The collection twists and turns purposefully between quiet moments with her daughter and dog and interlocutors as diverse as Anna Akhmatova, Homer, and Wadih Sa'adeh. Evoking intimacy over time and space, Lisa Stice's poems snuggle and spark, warm and rend, as her unfailing eye paints again and again that which should be against that which war takes away. She herself crafts the epithet for the task she's undertaken here: 'One-who-assembles-all-the-dismantled-parts.' I celebrate Stice for the quiet piercing of her needle-images and the healing tautness of the collection's narrative thread."

—Liam Corley, author of *Unwound: Poems from Enduring Wars*

Letters from Conflict

Poems

by
Lisa Stice

Middle West Press LLC
Johnston, Iowa

❖ ❖ ❖

Poetry / Witness to Conflict / Family & War

Letters from Conflict: Poems
ISBN (Print): 978-1-953665-26-3
ISBN (Kindle e-book): 978-1-953665-27-0
Library of Congress Catalog Number: 2024931269

❖ ❖ ❖

Middle West Press LLC
P.O. Box 1153
Johnston, Iowa 50131-9420
www.middlewestpress.com

❖ ❖ ❖

*Special thanks to Aiming Circle patrons
James Burns of Colorado Springs, Colorado
Nathan Didier of Cedar Falls, Iowa
Tim Lynch of McAllen, Texas*

Your patronage helps publish great military-themed writing!
www.aimingcircle.com

❖ ❖ ❖

*Cover image: V-mail operation in the field at APO 929, Port Moresby,
Papua New Guinea. 1944. Gift of John M. Lynes Sr. on behalf of
Mary T. Lynes, WAC, National World War 2 Museum, New Orleans*

Author photo by Andria Williams

For Saoirse and Seamus

Contents

Artist's Statement

When I was a kid, my parents gifted me an appreciation for the people and events that came before me. Before I could even read, I browsed the pictures of the *Time-Life Encyclopedia of the Old West*. We watched black-and-white films on videocassettes, and historical documentaries on PBS. We visited art and natural history museums. I listened to the stories of older relatives and family friends.

In short, history has always been very much a part of my present.

In previous poetry collections, including *Uniform*, *Permanent Change of Station*, and *FORCES*, I have variously experimented with erasures of military texts, recontextualized language from children's literature and Sun Tzu's *The Art of War,* and generated ekphrastic reactions to visual artwork.

The inspiration for *Letters from Conflict* came after reading a biography of British writer and poet Edward Thomas (1878-1917). Thomas was killed in World War I, and is sometimes labelled a war poet. The scope of his life's work exceeds the battlefield, however: He was also a critic, a biographer, and a writer of nature and travel. (Ironically, Thomas enlisted in the British Army at the age of 36, inspired by his correspondence with his American friend and contemporary Robert Frost, who had shared with Thomas an advance copy of the poem "The Road Not Taken.")

In his words and life story, Edward Thomas had seemed to me a lost and lonely soul. I thought he might be comforted if he had a letter in his pocket, even in the afterlife. So I wrote him one—as a poem.

I couldn't stop with just one such epistle-poem, however. There are so many other war writers—past and present—whose work I love. I decided to write them, too, hoping to show my gratitude for their insights and influences. Dear reader, we are each part of a wonderfully large community, a vast continuum of poetry-lovers.

We are each in conversation with one another.

—Lisa Stice,
March 2024

1

Dear Ciaran Carson

I write to you with fountain pen: a Waterman 52, circa 1920—
black with a nickel clip, classic, vintage, with a New York imprint
nib newly tuned, an even wear in the spot it rested
on another's hand and now leans easy against mine—
I tell you this because I know you know it's important, details,
where things come from—the pen is US made, like me.
How unexpected the weight: cataloguing people with whom
we share meals, people who work and come home late evening,
people who walked out of this life and sleep in retold memories—
mapping out cities and towns in words and punctuation: commas
where we snapped pictures in front of statues or signs or such,
semicolons at the spot between being couples and being families,
periods when we said goodbye and didn't know it was for good,
dead ends where we turned ourselves around an em dash—
The choosing of sides, divisions, buildings, destructions
appear elegant, written out in cursive or calligraphy, laid out
neat in even rows, fitted inside margins—

LISA STICE

Changing to the Major's Dress Blues

This uniform is different from the last
ten years. This one settles the heart.
Your thick brocades of gold,
age-forgiving cummerbund,
(more bravado than anything else)
are like nearing something:
we call it, *career*: spent in training for
combat zones and long silences.

This is the turning point—
for all these memories of pinning ribbons,
lining up medals, turning buttons,
making certain they're straight,

so that one day we will retire them to a bag
in a closet next to my evening gowns.

Dear Bruce Weigl

Bamboo grows three feet in a day.
I read that somewhere and now
it comes to mind how much we grow
with each day's passing, with each
face we pass or kiss or turn away—
if we could measure it, I think we'd
realize our hands can hold the sun,
already we cut down bamboo stalks,
make good use of all that hollowness.

The First Beginning

Imagine this: a photograph
two inches before your eyes:
a field of wildflowers,
Dad's impractical first car,

you before you walked,
or something entirely
not related to you,
an unnamed thing.

And how everything changes:
remember how this dog
was named Dog
and now is Seamus Jr.?

Remember how you could not
reach the top drawer?
Now you choose your clothes,
get dressed for the day.

I ask, *Who are you?*
and you say, *Big girl.*
I'm big and little
at the same time.

Dear Virgil

Yours is my favorite of the epics.
I suppose it could be for the fierce
storm that blows the ship to fate,
the fearful retelling of that giant
wooden horse with its belly full
of ambush, the bleeding tree of
prophecy, Dido's love and Juno's
bitter schemes, festivities and races,
arriving at a new shore, filling stomachs
with the fruit of promise, weapons
forged in Vulcan's furnace, ships
burning in the harbor, battle for
the fortress, negotiations for peace,
witnessing the birth of an empire,
but it isn't for all that. I love your
epic most because it is about
community, keeping people close.

In Our Backyard

We are camping
and telling stories.
This is our daughter's:

Once upon a time,
there was a dog.
His name was Seamus.
He was afraid of kitty-cats,
then he wasn't afraid of kitty-cats.
He slept with me
in my sleeping bag.

This is a tale of courage,
about the bravery she sees:

> her dog herding her
> to the room across
> from the vacuum cleaner
>
> feeling his shaking
> while he sits in front
> of her during thunder
>
> the sound of his sniff
> and scratch at the door
> during the night

When it is time for sleep,
he lies along her side
to take away the chill.

Dear Henry Reed

The bees are at war with the flowers this morning,
and so I think of you and wonder how to name
the parts of my life: We call this building a home,
but it isn't ours, borrowed walls and roof, a place
in between movement. And my husband has a billet,
all the duties therewith—what's my assignment then?
One-who-assembles-all-the-dismantled-parts
seems too awkward a title. And there are friends
I name faraway-friends and friends whose names
fade away after time. But these flowers are always
gardenias, these always pansies no matter the yard
where bees drone their hum-drum battle cries.

This Is the Year

the roses will never lose
their pink or drop a petal
to the ground

a permanent home
for hummingbirds and
bees and us

we will open our arms
let sunlight fill the open
spaces in between

welcome each day, familiar
as the last and feel safe
in the knowing

Dear Pablo Neruda

This is an ode to you,
rebel writer
with courage to defy
a father
a politic
an ideology
to write at ten
and to never stop
the lines
from slinking
across the page
of love
and life
in Chile
or in exile
on the move
across continents.

Ode to Haircuts

to the high and tight
faded on the sides
scissors and clippers
every Sunday afternoon
sideburns and face
smooth with faint dots
a razor every morning

to the wild toddler mane
bangs that peek and poke
eyes and mingle with lashes
the first cutting in an envelope
in a book in the closet
to look at later as a piece
of babyhood long gone

to the easy smoothness
as I pull my fingers through
that feeling that something
has left and what will come
will be thinner more dull
to the scattered auburn
mixed with gray around
my chair to mark another year

Dear Randy Brown, AKA "Charlie Sherpa"

it's the part about
coming home that reads
like a neighborly wave

so familiar, like how
State Fairs are always
crowds and funnel cake and noise

how someone I have met
in person only twice
can become a friend

your book on my shelf in
North Carolina, my book
on your shelf in Iowa

At Home

to see what you see
reflected
glittering and young

she gathers pine cones
not minding the sharp points
carrying as many
as she can in the small cradle
of her bare arms

we didn't realize the year slipping behind us
all the thoughts that now have words
how her hands will never again be this small

the dog makes his nest
pine needles pushed aside
a cool place to sleep
until we call *come in now*
come be our pet, you wild thing

Dear Phillis Wheatley

With your pen, you gathered the heavens,
pinned those celestial bodies to the page,
controlled the gods and made them speak,
ordered them serve for the good of us all.

If we woke each morning to your verse,
how good this world would be
to never hold anyone captive again,
instead to *shield their souls from harm.*

The Birds Began to Sing

I'd like to believe
there's much good

that jelly handprints
always wash off easily
from walls and furniture

that dogs always fetch
the ball and bring it back
with their tails wagging

that strangers always
smile when they pass
each other on the sidewalk

that children are taught
right from wrong and parents
always model *I'm sorry*

Dear Manju Kanchuli

How then do we plot this uneven course:
count the minutes and hours, string
them together to remind us of the faithfulness
of chronological time lest we lose track
when a day can feel like an entire year,

or do we mark the way with the stones
of our memory, quartz for the joys
and the ones made smooth by the river
for all those trials that wore us down,

or is it that we have no choice but to follow
the unpredictable winding and currents
of the river itself, risk drowning each time
we foolishly believe we have control?

Seek 'til You Find It

this is where I dreamt
the same dream each
night—minor details
sometimes changed—
walking into the ocean
stepping into a pool
letting a lake swallow
me whole—pausing
to turn and smile—
I'd see myself
like I was smiling
at myself—gathering
the water about me
like a sheet you discover
later—damp, molded

Dear Randall Jarrell

Yes, I understand what you mean about well water
and why letters should be burned. How comfort
comes with routine. How the past lingers behind
until we use it for kindling to warn us. And yet
we have so little choice in direction. Sometimes
endings don't come out so happy when rewriting
fairy tales. Old voices still whisper from ashes
that no amount of water can wash away.

In a Pumpkin Shell

We pass through two guarded gates, ID checks,
special passes, our names confirmed on a list.

    Marines escort us to a spot in the woods
    where POWs were kept. 80-year-old coils

of concertina wire holding us a captive audience
this family day. Here they keep us very well

    as we eat hot dogs, chips and sugar cookies
    before demonstrations of how husbands and

daddies build shelters of branches and dead leaves—
wives and children on the perimeter of secrets.

    Then at the close, two boys crawl into the dome
    of a shelter to make-believe at missing in action.

Dear Vera Brittain

When the men go away, the sky is blue, but
sometimes grays and it rains or snows. The wind
sometimes moves through the trees
making the sound of cascading water, or
the air is still and lets the sun warm your skin.

After the men return, the sky is blue, but
sometimes grays and it rains or snows. The wind
sometimes moves through the trees
making the sound of cascading water, or
the air is still and lets the sun warm your skin.

A Discount Store Breaks Ground

men arrive to fell the trees today
with machines, mostly yellow,
an unnatural yellow against
the rough bark of loblolly pines

and those trees forty feet high
and those trees newly sprouted
dragged away to flatbed trailers
gone, just like that

        we hear it
the booms and crashes
our dog paces the length of the room
our daughter asks, *what's that noise*

and already more progress
new machines scrape away
layers of soil, those weeds
with the little purple flowers

Dear Frank G. Gross

Do you think their souls are still there, too,
the ones whose bodies never left the mountains?
Did their spirits climb to the precipice,
touch the very edge of heaven? Or,
are they among the hills, some frozen mid-step,
some huddled together, some hugging
their own knees and never finding warmth?
Or, did they travel the long way home,
now sit hearthside each night of the first frost?

It Is Cold this Hour

I feel it when I open the blinds,
peer out, see how the streetlight
makes the moisture on glass
glow as if it creates its own
incandescence. On the sofa now,
I wrap the throw about me,
invite our dog to lie on my lap,
which he does, curls his body
into a tight ball. Our daughter
still sleeps, and I imagine her
deep steady breaths, imagine
her under her blankets and
a stuffed animal in each arm.
We are all warm in this house,
but you have already left and
forgotten your coat on the chair.

Dear Mzi Mahola

Then/now how country/cities/towns/streets
divide themselves into this-belongs-to-one,
this-belongs-to-the-other. So that children
on one side of a bridge must look across
decipher from a distance smiles/snarls.

I too am an *angered poet* after growing up
from my cul-de-sac youth, learning that
was/is. I call you strong/hope/brave poet
for safe-guarding your idea twelve years,
for fusing the continents with your words.

November 9, 2016

Yesterday, when I asked
my daughter what snack
she wanted, she told me
something she could share
with her dog.
        I sliced an apple
cut it into even chunks. One
for her, one for him, one for her
one for him. Until it was all gone
and the plate was empty.

Dear Sor Juana Inés de la Cruz

How I admire you—your battles
in this long war for women—
to study, to write, to teach,
to know *nothing unbound*
as our human intellect. And I know
you kept writing, even when
they took the materials away—
you must have at least composed
on the parchment of your mind
and whispered verse in place
of penance prayers.

Sugar and Spice

we are at ease
these days

coloring
inside the lines
(mostly)

picking up
our toys
right back
where they belong
(for the most part)

kneeling at our beds
closing our eyes
saying our prayers
(as much as can be expected)

Dear Tarfia Faizullah

I wept because your book had to be written
because there are children in this world
who have never known innocence who
no longer have mothers or sisters because
even those who liberate take away.
I wept because there are men who only
see women as things to use, vessels
in which to spill all their aggression.
I wept because there are 200,000 women
in one place alone (and who can say
how many more all about us) who
wash and scrub their skin raw but
will never feel clean again.

If You Haven't Any Daughters

you may not understand
why we do not tell them
that boy who just hit you
did that because he likes you

why we say *no thank you*
to the old man who offers
them a dollar at the bagel shop
the one who calls them *pretty things*

why we teach them self-
defense, math, science,
self-expression of words,
how to say *no* with command

why we hold tighter
their hands in ours

Dear Elie Wiesel

I cannot forget the sickness in my throat,
the heaviness in my core when I learned
that in 1939, nine-hundred Jewish refugees
on the *MS St. Louis*—a ship named
for the patron saint against the death
of children—cabled ahead, but the president
did not respond because he feared
they would take jobs from his own
and so the ship was turned away.

But I am sorry
others have forgotten.

Honey Is Sweeter than Blood

and yet, we bleed each other

    and yet

        and yet

           and yet

Dear Fred Marchant

If you hadn't signed all of those forms,
stood before that corporal's desk
for the last time, if you hadn't written
about all that, I still might be frozen
sitting at my desk with a pen in hand
and a journal open to blank pages.

When Marrying the Corps

honor and privilege, a round of applause
thank you for sharing your loved one
part of our larger family now
loyalty, love, support: your sacrifice

from the parade deck to the years to come
willingness to march forward, to stand up
committed to give critical time
set yourself apart from personal wishes

you will wonder what kind of hell this is
at a day's notice that he leaves tonight
the conversations you started but did not finish
proving to others that you can fight on your own

you have infiltrated the dream we all share
the bond that shapes everything you do

Dear Federico García Lorca

From my window, I cannot see
them, but I know lonely people
travel this night in darkness.

Are you at their sides? Reciting
verses? Did you stand up
from the spot you fell, simply
brushed the sand from your clothes?

Under moonlight, across sea
and land. Perhaps you heard
my sigh and felt this quiet here.

The Other Bird Flew After

what is that sound
coming through the trees
this autumn twilight

sad and far away
like cries of mourning doves
song deep in their chests

Dear Judith Wright

My daughter had that nightmare again
(this is five nights in a row now),
and when I ask her what it was about,
she lacks the words to tell me
or maybe she remembers only the fear
and the waking and her all alone.
I tell her *it is only our past and future
troubling your sleep*, then she nods
and I wipe away her tears because
that is all we can do in this moment.

In the Dark

she has handed me her favorite dog
the one that looks just like
our real dog, but this one never barks

    it sleeps with her at night
    held tight in her arms, pulled against
    her soft cheek: recipient of song

    of murmured wishes as sleep
    comes heavy under night light glow
    dreams warmed by blankets

but now, she hands him over
says she wants to share with me
because it is scary to sleep alone

Dear Edward Thomas

On cold mornings, when moisture collects
on the windows, your lines crawl into memory,
and my lips make the silent motion of words.
Cold, even with a heater on, I move across
the room and take your book from its shelf.
Know that I love you from place and time
far away. Blessed are you this cold, wet morning;
blessed am I as I slip back under the blanket,
turn your pages, warmed like poppies
opened to the sunshine of spring.

At Bedtime During Deployment

I miss him, she says
and I say, so do I
we will see him again
I love him, she says

and I say, so do I
distance feels further
I love him, she says
further in quiet moments

distance feels further
memory like a mirage
further in quiet moments
how time seems to stop

memory like a mirage
I love him, she says
how time seems to stop
I miss him, she says

Dear Emily Dickinson

My husband is away—my daughter is at school—
the dog is at the groomer—and this quiet feels so heavy

I can see it. It looks like you. You seated in a chair—
in your room where you watch from your window

the soldiers' deliberate march past the garden—
off to somewhere far away not like the poems

that stay close to home—travel with pies and Valentines—
the men travel over the hills—while you wait

as if you truly believe they will all return—
but you hear it in the silence—a truth without slant—

How Does Your Garden Grow

with the wildest seeds
scattered by hand

with months of heavy rain

with watering cans
carried back and forth
from the spigot
between storms

with hummed tunes
to bumble bees

with a promise

with waiting
and waiting
and waiting

Dear Nazim Hikmet

Are you wandering, still, a country not your own,
far from the ones you love, in exile all alone?

Are you an eternal passenger on a train in winter
with no one seated next to you, alone?

Or, are you in a cold cell with your verse
and your letters, reading them alone?

How time must distort when gazing
at a photograph thirteen years old, alone.

How thirty years away from what you know
must make you think you will always be alone.

Please, I would like to believe she is next to you
and you are home, no longer alone.

This Is the Way

the glaciers recede
slowly—a sliding
grinding of earth—
an erosion we see
in the ridges of rock
and the gray-blue water

we are on a tour
you are in Daddy's arms
I snap a picture
as you point at icebergs
and tell their shapes
that one's an eagle

this is the way we age
slowly—a sliding
grinding of earth—
you: pushing away
Daddy: bending, opening his arms
me: reaching for your hand

Dear Hadraawi

I ask my husband to tell me
of his deployment to Somaliland.

He says, in the morning
camels were lowered from cargo ships
by cranes, the huge animals
secured in harnesses and sat gently
on the ground to be herded away,
during the day long camel trains
walked along the roads to the horizon,
and the night air carried
the smell of burning camel flesh.

War

peacekeeping missions:
with shouldered rifles
flak vests and armored trucks
night patrols and guard-posts
candy and tobacco in pockets

melee in the streets: gathered
crowds with phones, record
scuffle and commotion
onlookers retreat with
blood on their shoes

disputes: battled out in heated
discussions with words lobbed
across the dinner table or
the living room sofa in front
of the television and kids

games played by children:
with cards flipped face-up
thumb to thumb combat
good guys vs. bad guys
the winner gloats victory

Dear Kathleen Flenniken

Isn't it funny how yardsticks measure height,
pencils make hashmarks on a doorjamb,
but whole years live in the empty spaces?
So much is said in the not-saying—and how
those things we can't see really do hurt us.
We could ride our bike up and down the same
driveway, day after day, our entire childhood,
and never see the uneven spot that could send
us flying if the tire hit it just right, but
it didn't matter anyway because our moms
healed anything with a Band-Aid and a kiss.

At the Atomic Museum

In the 1950s, Nevada test-site engineers were told
there would be no long-term effects from
the experiments. The government praised them
for their patriotism in Christmas cards to each family.
The men collected and carried home souvenir
uranium rods to show their kids and wives.
At the Atomic Museum, I read copies of denial letters—
    "Dear Mrs. S----,
    We are sorry for your loss.
    To help put your mind at ease,
        our research finds no correlation
        between your husband's work
        environment and his lymphoma."
    and once confidential files—
    "S---- received 891 rads of neutron radiation,
nearly a lethal dose. His badge will be kept
in a lead box in the case further tests are warranted."

My brother gave me a Vaseline Glass candy dish
last year for Christmas. It glows
under black light. Who owned it
when it was just a lovely novelty?
Maybe a woman with a courted daughter.
The girl might have sat on the couch with her sweet
as they ate sugary treats out of the dish.
Would the candy glow under black light, too?
Maybe the mother gave the girl the yellow glass
as a wedding gift, each lemon drop and ribbon candy
dissolving into syrupy malignance.

The museum's display of vintage TVs loop,

duck-and-cover commercials: *If you see a flash,*
lie face down on the ground and throw dirt over yourself.
Just in case no one would be left behind to dig a grave?
If you see a flash, hide behind something like a tree.
Photographs show refrigerators used as shields,
like tombstones, sitting in the desert sand.

Kids in southern Utah ran outside, excited
to see snow fall in July. They held up their hands
and stuck out their tongues to catch
the falling ash, rolled in mounds on the ground,
threw handfuls at each other. Frolicking in the wonder
of it all, they never hid from the flash they didn't see.

I read about the uses of mill tailings and watch newsreels
of construction workers pouring radioactive cement
for the foundation of a school,
such an industrious solution for all that waste.

My hometown was built on mill tailings. Before I was born,
crews broke up and removed old foundations
and replaced them with less tainted cement, but
contaminated water still ran through irrigation ditches
to water cornfields and asparagus patches, and
contaminated water ran through our kitchen pipes.
Five members from little St. Ann's Church were diagnosed
with brain tumors in 2007. My uncle's neighbor had a tumor
on his spine, tangled around nerves.

I browse through the gift shop at toy Geiger counters,
Glo Sticks, DVDs of the duck-and-cover
tutorials. I spin the postcard rack and carry home a souvenir
picture of sunglassed men posing in front of a mushroom cloud,
safe and still smiling.

Dear Cho Chi-hun

I broke open a pomegranate,
how satisfying the crack of outer shell,
opening to chambers and arteries
and those sweet pockets of seeds.
The red juice ran over my hands
and dripped into the sink—*like blood*—
I thought—*romantic*.

Veterans Cemetery

a lovely picture—
no trees, a clean lawn evenly

mowed, uniformity of stones
laid out on a grid, each

marker numbered, lined up
in military formation, like

new pieces of chalk before
the lesson begins, hash-marks

keep track of what's won or
lost, *how perfectly peaceful*

this order that feels so natural
what we've come to expect

Dear Wadih Sa'adeh

Yes, we work with what we have
attempt to shape the world around us,
but I am not talented enough
to paint new constellations or
to build happy people here or
to build happy people and send them
some other place which needs them more.

But I have made a bowl, thick sided,
have placed it in the spot between
my heart and my stomach, and
I place in it all the silences it can hold.

Changes Can Occur

Let us know
if you have questions   concerns.
We will be here

if you would like help with
past   present   or future
to build your happily-ever-after military life:

make an appointment now.
Paperwork required,
completed on time.

Only couples without complex problems
will be seen due to strict schedules.
We apologize for any inconvenience.

Thank you.

Dear Victoria Kelly

I understand what it's like when our men go away,
when we are left behind with the chore
of keeping a dailiness, a routine. And how,
when we are washing dishes or folding laundry,
something so in this world takes us out of this world.
How removed we feel. How distant our friends seem.
How quiet the house is in the morning.
We leave for the market and come back home,
and the next day, we go somewhere else
and come back home while our men are still away.

They'll Come Home

they'll drop their rucks at the door
we'll hug
they'll say, *I missed you*
we'll say, *I missed you, too*

then, there will be quiet
and awkwardness
they'll feel like they need
to say something, but
they won't know what to say,

and we won't know what to say
partly because nothing comes to mind
partly because we feel guilty for having fun
partly because they are unfamiliar

then, the quiet will linger
a little while longer

LISA STICE

Dear Anna Akhmatova

I read your song for the dead,
then shut my eyes and see—
you and all those women
standing in line outside the gates
keeping vigil for the release of
fathers, brothers, sons.

Over those long months waiting,
icy winds fade youthfulness of face,
smother the flames of the eyes,
crack lips until speaking pains,
until women on their death watch
become shells, look somewhat like
who they used to be.

She Is Correct

Over the phone the other day,
I spoke with a friend.
She said, *You've changed
so much. You're not the same
as you were before.*

Dear Wislawa Szymborska

As I sit in the dim, blue light of the television,
while my daughter sleeps in her room and
my husband dozes on the floor, my dog leans
his head against my leg. A warmth
that vanishes any trace of cold, much like
that first sip of hot cocoa at the first sign
of frost. This will be the last evening of its kind
for a while. The next, I will sit in the dim,
blue light of the television, my daughter
will sleep in her room, the dog will lean his head
against my leg, while my husband sleeps somewhere
in a field (maybe under a tent, maybe not).
We adjust well, *are doing just fine.*
Still part of a whole as the experiment claims.
I think I am happy. Would you call this happiness?

Puppy Dog Tails

here are two ears:
    see how they move independently
    search for that familiar cadence
    anticipate the key in the lock

here is a nose:
    see how it twitches
    isolates aftershave and sweat
    knows who is coming up the walk

here is a tongue:
    see how it hangs and drips
    hungry for someone else
    to take over watch of this house

here is a tail:
    see how it moves slow then fast
    in recognition of memories
    a metronome to the tune of homecoming

here are four paws:
    see how they dance
    hear how the nails click on the floor
    see how they root now for the pounce

here is a body:
    see how it wriggles
    ready to be lifted into the air
    then later sleep on Daddy's warm chest

Dear Homer

O composer of epics, chronicles
of heroes as they're seen through children's eyes.
You must have told us of Odysseus
as Telemachus saw him: taller than
the trees themselves, smarter than the scholars,
slayer of monsters, master of the sea.
A child believes his father will return
and even when tied to the mast, can calm
the wildest tempests, loudest furies.

Buttons Round and Sound and Pretty

round, you say, *like circle*
yes, I say and show you
how to turn each button
make the eagle stand straight
the earth anchor itself

how easy it is to set this brass
in order, to iron wrinkles
out of wool, roll tape
around our hands to pat
away rogue fluff and lint

I say, *how handsome Daddy looks*
wonder if you see a man
or someone who flies
without wings, circles
the earth before returning home

Dear Sun Tzu

1. You taught me what's important.
2. That everything is always at odds. Us and them,
   this and that, pushing against each other.
3. We are either building encampments
   or on the move, gathering what we can.
4. There are the things we need like clothing
   for different climates, beds for sleeping,
   photo albums for helping us remember
   where we were and who we used to be.

We Were Not Here

it is moving day—
no one kisses us goodbye
there are only orders
telling us where to go

we don't wake
to cups of Earl Grey
no spoonfuls
of sugar stirred in

we don't sit down
to bacon and eggs
over easy   or even
cold cereal and milk

we don't leave
dirty dishes piled
in the sink or anything
else that needs cleaning up

Acknowledgements

I am grateful to the editors of the following literary magazines, in which these poems first appeared—some in slightly different versions:

"At Bedtime During Deployment" *As You Were* Vol. 5, Fall/Winter 2016

"At Home" first stanza from *Ink in Thirds* "TLT Throwback" on-line feature No. 26; third stanza from *Ink in Thirds* "TLT Throwback" on-line feature No. 29; 2016

"At the Atomic Museum" *Nuclear Impact: Broken Atoms in Our Hands* (Shabda Press, 2017)

"Buttons Round and Sound and Pretty" *The Sea Letter* No. 3 summer 2018

"Changes Can Occur" *O-Dark-Thirty: The Review* Vol. 5, No. 2, Winter 2017

"Changing to the Major's Dress Blues" *As You Were* Vol. 5, Fall/Winter 2016

"Dear Cho Chi-hun" *Poems-For-All* #1637, October 2021

"Dear Ciaran Carson" *A New Ulster* issue No. 58 July 2017

"Dear Edward Thomas" *Moledro Magazine* No. 4, December 2016

"Dear Emily Dickinson" *Moledro Magazine* No. 4, December 2016

"Dear Elie Wiesel" *Poetry Super Highway's* 19th annual Yom Hashoah (Holocaust Remembrance Day) issue April 2017

"**Dear Federico García Lorca,**" *The Galway Review* Jan. 4, 2017

"**Dear Henry Reed,**" first appeared in *The Deadly Writers Patrol* No. 13, Fall 2017

"**Dear Homer**" *As You Were* Vol. 7 Fall/Winter 2017

"**Dear Judith Wright**" *Collateral* Vol. 2, No. 1 autumn 2017

"**Dear Kathleen Flenniken**" *The Galway Review* Jan. 4, 2017

"**Dear Nazim Hikmet**" *Moledro Magazine* No. 4, December 2016

"**Dear Randall Jarrell**" *The Deadly Writers Patrol* No. 13, Fall 2017

"**Dear Vera Brittain**" *The Tishman Review* Vol. 3, No. 3, Summer 2017

"**Dear Wadih Sa'adeh**" *Proud to Be: Writing by American Warriors* Vol. 6 November 2017 (Southeast Missouri State University Press, 2017) *Selected as an honorable mention in poetry.*

"**Dear Wislawa Szymborska**" *The Tishman Review* Vol. 3, No. 3 Summer 2017

"**If You Haven't Any Daughters**" *The Rise Up Review* July 2017

"**It Is Cold this Hour**" *The Deadly Writers Patrol* No. 13, Fall 2017

"**In a Pumpkin Shell** " *The Deadly Writers Patrol* No. 13, Fall 2017

"**The Other Bird Flew After,**" *The Galway Review* Jan. 4, 2017

"**Puppy Dog Tails**" *Paw Prints in Verse: Poems about Pets* (Poetry Contests for a Cause, 2017)

"**Seek 'til You Find It**" *Foliate Oak Literary Magazine* December 2018

"**This Is the Way**" *Luminous Echoes: A Poetry Anthology* (*Into the Void Magazine*, 2017)

"**This Is the Year**" first appeared in *The Galway Review* Jan. 4, 2017

"**We Were Not Here**" *Peeking Cat Poetry Magazine* No. 21, January 2017

"**When Marrying the Corps**" *Poetry Leaves: Waterford Township Public Library* on exhibit May 2-31, 2017

Notes on Poems

To ensure full disclosure and translation, I give credit here to the words, people, events, and art that inspired my own, as well as the conflicts from which they bore witness and grew.

"The Birds Began to Sing": title from the nursery rhyme "Sing a Song of Sixpence"

"Buttons Round and Sound and Pretty": title from the nursery rhyme "Buttons"

"Dear Anna Akhmatova" **(1889-1966)**: Russian Revolution; author of Selected Poems, translated by D. M. Thomas (Penguin Books, 1985)

"Dear Bruce Weigl" **(1949-)**: Vietnam War veteran (U.S.), author of *Song of Napalm* (Atlantic Monthly Press, 1994)

"Dear Ciaran Carson" **(1948-2019)**: The Troubles in Northern Ireland; author of several collections including *The Irish for No* (Wake Forest University Press, 1987)

"Dear Cho Chi-hun" **(1920-1968)**: Korean War veteran (South Korean Army), author of several poems in *Brother Enemy: Poems of the Korean War*, edited and translated by Suh Ji-Moon (White Pine Press, 2002)

"Dear Edward Thomas" **(1878-1917)**: World War I; author of The Annotated Collected Poems (Bloodaxe Books, 2009)

"Dear Elie Wiesel" **(1928-2016)**: World War II and The Holocaust; author of *Night* (Bantam Books, 1982); contributor to *Holocaust Poetry* compiled by Hilda Schiff (St. Martin's Griffin, 1995)

"Dear Emily Dickinson" (1830-1886): American Civil War; author of *The Complete Poems of Emily Dickinson* (Back Bay Books, 1976)

"Dear Federico García Lorca" (1898-1936): Spanish Civil War; author of *The Selected Poems of Federico García Lorca* (New Directions, 2005)

"Dear Frank G. Gross" (1930-2021): Korean War veteran. (U.S.); author of Frank G. Gross Collection (AFC/2001/001/27374), Veterans History Project, American Folklife Center, Library of Congress

"Dear Fred Marchant" (1946-): Vietnam War; author of *The Looking House: Poems* (Graywolf Press, 2009); italicized words from "Conscientious Objector Discharge"

"Dear Hadraawi": Maxamed Ibraahin Warsame (1943-2022); Poet of the Somali Civil War; 2012 Prince Claus Award winner

"Dear Henry Reed" (1914-1986): World War II veteran (U.K.); author of *Henry Reed: Collected Poems* (Carcanet Press Ltd., 2007)

"Dear Kathleen Flenniken" (1960-): The Cold War; author of *Plume* (University of Washington Press, 2012)

"Dear Homer" (751 BCE-651 BCE, estimated): Trojan War; author of *The Odyssey*

"Dear Judith Wright" (1915-2000): Aboriginal land rights activist in Australia; author of A *Human Pattern: Selected Poems*, selected by Judith Wright (Fyfield Books, 2011); italicized words taken and altered from "The Trains"

"Dear Manju Kanchuli" **(1951-):** Nepalese Civil War; contributor for *Language for a New Century,* edited by Tina Chang, Nathalie Handal, and Ravi Shankar (W. W. Norton, 2008)

"Dear Mzi Mahola" **(1949-):** South African Apartheid and Soweto Uprising, author of *Dancing in the Rain: A Collection of Poetry* (University of KwaZulu-Natal Press, 2006)

"Dear Nazim Hikmet" **(1902-1963):** Turkish War of Independence and Russian Revolution; author of *Poems of Nazim Hickmet,* 2nd Edition, translated by Randy Blasing and Mutlu Konuch (Persea Books, 2002)

"Dear Pablo Neruda" **(1904-1973):** Spanish Civil War and World War II; author of *Full Woman, Fleshly Apple, Hot Moon,* translated by Stephen Mitchell (Harper Perennial, 2009)

"Dear Phillis Wheatley" **(1753-1784):** American Revolution; author of *Phillis Wheatley, Complete Writings* (Penguin Classics, 2001); italicized words from "A Farewell to America"

"Dear Randall Jarrell" **(1914-1965):** World War II veteran (U.S.); author of several collections including *The Complete Poems* (Farrar, Straus & Giroux, 1981)

"Dear Randy Brown ..." **(1968-):** Operation Enduring Freedom veteran (U.S.); author of *Welcome to FOB Haiku: War Poems from Inside the Wire* (Middle West Press LLC, 2015)

"Dear Sor Juana Inés de la Cruz" **(1651-1695):** colonial Mexico; author of *Sor Juana Inés de la Cruz: Poems,* translated by Margaret Sayers Peden (Bilingual Press, 1985); italicized words from "Prologue to the Reader"

LISA STICE

"Dear Sun Tzu" (544 BCE-496 BCE): turbulent late Chou dynasty; author of The *Art of War*

"Dear Tarfia Faizullah" (1980-): Pakistani Liberation War of Bangladesh 1971; author of *Seam* (Southern Illinois University Press, 2014)

"Dear Wadih Sa'adeh" (1948-): Lebanese Civil War and other conflicts; contributor for *Language for a New Century,* edited by Tina Chang, Nathalie Handal, and Ravi Shankar (W. W. Norton, 2008)

"Dear Wislawa Szymborska" (1923-2012): World War II; author of *View with a Grain of Sand: Selected Poems* (Harcourt Brace, 1995); italicized words from "Experiment"

"Dear Vera Brittain" (1893-1970): World War I; anthologized in *Scars Upon My Heart: Women's Poetry and Verse of the First World War*, selected by Catherine Reilly (Virago, 1981)

"Dear Victoria Kelly": Operation Enduring Freedom; author of *When the Men Go Off to War: Poems* (Naval Institute Press, 2015) and *Homefront* (University of Nevada Press, 2024)

"Dear Virgil" (70 BCE-19 BCE): Trojan War veteran; author of *The Aeneid*

"The First Beginning": title from the nursery rhyme "That's All"

"Honey Is Sweeter than Blood": title from the Salvador Dalí painting of the same name

"How Does Your Garden Grow": title from the nursery rhyme "Mary, Mary Quite Contrary"

"If You Haven't Any Daughters": title from the nursery rhyme "Hot Cross Buns"

"In a Pumpkin Shell": title from the nursery rhyme "Peter, Peter Pumpkin Eater"

"The Other Bird Flew After": title from the nursery rhyme "Two Birds"

"Puppy Dog Tails": title from the nursery rhyme "What Are Little Boys Made Of"

"Seek 'til You Find It": title from the nursery rhyme "For Every Evil"

"Sugar and Spice": title from the nursery rhyme "What Little Girls Are Made Of"

"They'll Come Home": title from the nursery rhyme "Little Bo Peep"

"This Is the Way": title from the nursery rhyme "This Is the Way We Tie Our Shoes"

A Few Words of Thanks

Thanks to my parents—Lois and Bob—for gifting me my love of books and history, for all their love and support, and for telling everyone they meet about my books.

Thanks to my brother—Paddy—for our imaginative childhood and for making me laugh with his wit.

Thanks to my husband for being my proof-reader and for proudly telling his fellow Marines about my poetry.

Thanks to my daughter—Saoirse—for being a quirky kiddo who inspires so much of my writing.

Thanks to my Norwich Terrier—Seamus—who patiently lies by my feet as I write or type.

Thanks to Middle West Press for turning my manuscript into a beautiful book.

Thanks to my fellow Middle West Press writers: Randy Brown, Eric Chandler, Amalie Flynn, Ben Weakly, Benjamin B. White, Ron Riekki, Jessi Atherton, Liam Corley, J.B. Stevens, and Aly Allen.

Thanks to my writer friends (too many to list) and to all my contemporary war writers and those who came before (especially way too many to list).

Thanks to Peter Molin founder of the *Time Now* blog; Andria Williams, founder of *The Military Spouse Book Review*; and Jess Goodin, founder of Military Spouse Fine Artists Network (MilspoFAN), for their support to writers and artists who share military experiences.

Thanks to the National World War II Museum, New Orleans, for the use of their archive photograph related to Victory Mail.

Thanks to all the poets who inspired these epistle poems.

Thanks to *Military Spouse Book Review*, Military Spouse Fine Artists Network, and Veterans Writing Project for offering me opportunities to actively help foster communities of military writers and artists.

Thanks to my literature and composition professors from Mesa State College (now Colorado Mesa University).

Thanks to my creative writing professors and fellow low-residency MFA students from the University of Alaska, Anchorage.

Thanks to the poets, writers, and artists who inspired these poems.

Thanks to the editors of literary journals who first published some of these poems.

Thanks to Middle West Press for letting these poems gather as a family.

Thanks to all those who read poetry.

Thanks to all those who read to children.

Thanks to anyone who still writes letters.

About the Writer

Lisa Stice is the author of the previously published poetry collections Uniform (Aldrich Press, 2016), *Permanent Change of Station* (Middle West Press, 2018), *FORCES* (Middle West Press, 2021), and the poetry chapbook *Desert* (Prolific Press, 2018). Her work appears widely in literary journals and anthologies worldwide, the latter including *Beyond the Hill* (Lost Tower Publications, 2017); and *Nuclear Impact: Broken Atoms in Our Hands* (Shabda Press, 2017).

Stice's poem "Pursuit" was the 2020 military-family category poetry winner in the Col. Darron L. Wright Memorial Writing Awards, administered annually by the literary journal *Line of Advance*.

In 2017, her poem "Dear Wadih Sa'adeh" was selected as an honorable mention in the poetry category in that year's volume of the *Proud to Be: Writing by American Warriors* anthology series, published by Southeast Missouri State University Press. Her poem "A Quick Lunch from the Noodle Stand" was nominated for a 2016 Pushcart Prize by *The Magnolia Review*. In 2022, she was awarded a "Poetry of Modern Conflict" prize by the non-profit Sangria Summit Society.

In 2023, Stice joined Middle West Press LLC as an associate editor. There, she was most-recently the co-editor of the 2023 anthology, *Things We Carry Still: Poems & Micro-Stories about Military Gear.* Stice is also poetry editor for *Inklette Magazine,* and often serves as an editor and mentor with various other writing organizations.

The poet holds a Bachelor of Arts in English literature from Mesa State College (now Colorado Mesa University), Grand Junction, Colorado, and a Master of Fine Arts in Creative Writing and Literary Arts from the University of Alaska, Anchorage.

She currently lives in North Carolina with her husband, daughter, and a beloved Norwich Terrier named Seamus.

You can learn more about her on-line at: lisastice.wordpress.com

Inspired? Thoughts & Prompts on Writing Epistolary Poems

How exciting it is to receive a letter in the mail! A letter, after all, takes time and thought. A letter is intimate and personal. Any letter is rare gift, in our busy digital age.

The word "epistolary" comes from the Latin *epistula*, which means letter. The form of epistolary poetry goes as far back as Ovid's (43 BCE-18 AD) *Epistulae Heroidum* ("Letters from Heroines")—a set of 15 poems written in various Greek and Roman heroic personas.

An epistle poem is usually in direct address to an actual person, but can also be written to an imagined character. Such poems need not follow any meter or rhyme pattern, and can be either be formal or colloquial.

Here are some further examples of the form:

- **Evie Shockley's (1965 -)** "from The Lost Letters of Frederick Douglass"
- **Major Jackson's (1968-)** "Letter to Brooks: Spring Garden"
- **Alexander Pope's (1688-1744)** "Epistle to Miss Blount, On Her Leaving the Town, After the Coronation"
- **Langston Hughes' (1901-1967)** "Mother to Son"
- **Meg Day's (1984-)** "Another Night at Sea Level"

Prompt No. 1: Think of an historical figure with whom you would like to have a philosophical conversation. Ask questions. Make connections among the conflicts, concerns, and challenges of your respective times.

Prompt No. 2: Is there a friend with whom you haven't spoken in a long while, maybe even a best friend from your youth? Compose an epistolary poem peppered with reminisces.

Prompt No. 3: Write an epistolary poem that calls for change. This can be to an individual or a group of people. Consider your addressees' beliefs and backgrounds. Shape the structure, tone, and style of your poem, to find common ground and purpose.

Also from Middle West Press LLC

anthologies

*Our Best War Stories: Prize-winning Poetry & Prose
from the Col. Darron L. Wright Memorial Awards*
Edited by Christopher Lyke

Things We Carry Still: Poems & Micro-Stories about Military Gear
Edited by Lisa Stice and Randy Brown

❖   ❖   ❖

poetry collections

Permanent Change of Station and *FORCES*
by Lisa Stice

Paying for Gas with Quarters: A Parent's Odyssey in Poems
by Aly Allen

The Time War Takes
by Jessi M. Atherton

Unwound: Poems from Enduring Wars
by Liam Corley

Hugging This Rock: Poems of Earth & Sky, Love & War
by Eric Chandler

September Eleventh: an epic poem, in fragments
by Amalie Flynn

HEAT + PRESSURE: Poems from War
by Ben Weakley